Heaven
Is it for REAL?

by Joe Crews

One

Is it for Real?

Millions of people are anticipating, although for different reasons, a time when they can leave this planet and migrate to another happier, less cluttered world in space. Many believe that time is running out for this overcrowded, polluted planet which has been so misused for 6,000 years. For survival purposes only, they hope to move into an orbiting satellite, made scientifically secure by fail-proof technology. There, in an artificially sustained, friendly environment, they hope to become pioneers of a new space world for restless earthlings.

Millions of others look heavenward and lay their exciting plans for more distant space travel, far beyond the edges of our solar system. Their expectations are not grounded in the scientific production of laboratory landscapes and recycled chemicals. They look for a space home totally independent of human error and influence; a home free of corrupting pride, selfishness, and sin; a home called heaven, which they believe is now in preparation for them. They expect to travel there long before the white-smocked scientist develops his satellite colony.

It is easy to empathize with those who are fed up with the distressing problems of planet earth and who want to immigrate to some more pleasing environment. But will the artificial conditions in a self-contained space colony be greatly superior to our worn-out earth? True, the chemically-created atmosphere could be more easily regulated and maintained, but what about the basic, ultimate problems of survival?

Death and disease can be no more avoided in space than they can right here. Crime and injustices would follow human beings wherever they might travel in the universe. Disappointments and heart-wrenching sorrow would continue to mark the brief course of human existence, simply because man's greatest problem is man himself. He cannot elude his own selfish nature by fleeing to another location—even to another planet. Neither can he escape from his mortality by changing environments.

What man really needs is a perfectly integrated, sinless nature that would not be subject to sickness or death, plus a perfect environment in which to live for eternity. Such an ideal arrangement is the only one that will solve all the problems and fulfill all the dreams of all the people in the world today. Perfect health, a beautiful home, an ideal climate, and eternal life—what else could anyone really wish for?

Could all these incredible conditions ever become a reality? The scientists say No. They can promise better health and a longer life span, but never immortality. They hope for cleaner air and improved working conditions, but no germ-free environment. That is the best they can do. But listen, there is a place now in preparation that will exceed all the extravagant words I have used in describing it. Most scientists deny its existence, because they don't believe there is a God who lives in a place called heaven.

Two
Back to the Original Plan

I want you to see that this future home now being prepared for us will actually fulfill God's original plan for man's perfect happiness. It will match the exquisite beauty and glory that God incorporated into the Garden of Eden. Isaiah described it this way: "For since the beginning of the world men have not heard, nor perceived by the ear, neither hath the eye seen, O God, beside thee, what he hath prepared for him that waiteth for him" (Isaiah 64:4).

The prophet here declares that "since the beginning of the world" men have neither heard nor seen the fullness of God's plan. The intimation is clear—men once did see, hear, and know of the wonderful things God has prepared for His people. In fact, that plan was revealed to Adam and Eve in all its glory. God wanted the earth to be like Eden, the Garden of the Lord. He gave four tremendous gifts to our first parents—life, a righteous character, a beautiful home, and dominion over the earth. They could have possessed those gifts forever by simply choosing to obey God in the matter of the one forbidden tree. Through obedience to His will, God intended to make the human family ideally and eternally happy.

Angels must have wept when they saw sin come into the human family for the first time. Immediately, all of those original provisions began to be withdrawn. Adam and Eve began to die according to the pronouncement of God; their dominion passed for the time into the hands of Satan; the image of righteousness was marred within them; and they were driven out of the garden home. The first three chapters of the Bible present the picture of this great loss. The entrance of sin and the story of the fall of man are graphically told in Genesis 1, 2, and 3. But the last three chapters of the Bible picture the exact opposite by telling of the restoration of all things. The exit of sin and Satan, and the removal of the curse are depicted in Revelation 20–22.

Now let me assure you that the home of the righteous is going to be right here on this earth. Jesus tells us this in Matthew 5:5. In giving His Beatitudes He said: "Blessed are the meek: for they shall inherit the earth." Mark it down well. God's people will finally dwell in this beautiful world, not as it is today, but as it shall be prepared for the saints.

This is really most natural when you think of it. God planned for His children to live here when He created the world. He placed our first parents in a paradise without spot or blemish. Now it is true that the devil came into the picture and interrupted God's plan, but he did not change that plan. God will finally carry out His great original purpose as it was revealed in the Garden of Eden. He will restore this earth to its first dominion. He will make it sinless and perfect again, and His people will live here in the beauty of Eden restored. The wicked today have more of the earth than the righteous, and I suppose the finance companies have more than both groups together. But some day, God says, the saints will inherit the earth.

Surely no one would want the earth in its present condition, because it's quite a mess now. We can thank the Lord that when He gives it back to us it will be altogether different from what we see around us today. In Isaiah 65:17 we read these beautiful words: "For, behold, I create new heavens and a new earth." That is the Old Testament account, but turn to the New Testament and you will read the same thing in Revelation 21:1: "And I saw a new heaven and a new earth."

This old blood-soaked world of ours will be replaced completely, and all trace of sin will be removed forever. Peter describes it in these words: "Nevertheless we, according to his promise, look for new heavens and a new earth, wherein dwelleth righteousness" (2 Peter 3:13). That is the kind of world I want—a world in which righteousness dwells! God is going to have a pure, clean planet again. Listen, if a man should neglect to take the opportunity to live there, he will commit the most colossal blunder of his life! That is the most tragic mistake anyone could ever make. May God help us to make that home a glorious assurance without fail.

It is shocking how many weak and twisted concepts of heaven people have accepted. Most folks think of it as some far off ethereal place—and that is about all the average man knows about heaven. He believes it is "up there" somewhere. Yes, it is "up there," and we can agree with him that far, for when Jesus went away, He went up (Acts 1:9). And He said: "I go to prepare a place for you. And if I go and prepare a place for you, I will come again, and receive you unto myself; that where I am, there ye may be also" (John 14:2, 3).

Please notice that Jesus called heaven a place. New York is a place, and heaven is going to be just as real as New York. Jesus declared that He is going to get a place ready and then come back to take us with Him to that place. This is not some ghostly, unreal idea. The righteous will not sit on clouds out there in space, playing harps and singing hallelujah choruses all during eternity. This is a very false and unbiblical picture of heaven.

The only reason a few people do not want to go to heaven is that they don't know what it will be like. You may find a person now and then who will tell you plainly that he doesn't care to go to heaven, but that is only because he has a misconception about it. Popular myths have made heaven seem dull and uninteresting.

The truth about heaven makes it one of the most exciting places imaginable. The capital city of that future glory land is called the New Jerusalem, and it is currently under construction according to the testimony of Jesus and Paul. It will cover an area greater than Virginia, the District of Columbia, Pennsylvania, New Jersey, and Rhode Island combined. If you find that unbelievable, don't take my word for it. Here it is in the Bible: "But now they desire a better country, that is, an heavenly: wherefore God is not ashamed to be called their God: for he hath prepared for them a city" (Hebrews 11:16). Here we are told that God is getting a city ready for His people. He is preparing one now.

This raises some questions. What kind of city is God building for His faithful ones? Where is it being made ready? Revelation 21:2 answers: "And I John saw the holy city coming down from God out of heaven." In paradise at this moment, far above the stars and planets, God is preparing mansions for you and me. Someday that gleaming white city will descend right down to the earth and settle here as the eternal home of the righteous. How big will it be on completion? Revelation 21:16 tells us: "And the city lieth foursquare, ... and he measured the city with the reed, twelve thousand furlongs."

You will notice that the city is perfectly square and the circumference is 12,000 furlongs, or 1,500 miles. Since a furlong is one-eighth of a mile, this means the city is 375 miles on each side. Believe it or not, 450 New York Cities could be placed inside its gigantic walls. The streets are pure gold, and the gates of it are solid pearl—not merely composed of pearls, but actually made of one solid pearl. Imagine, if you can, a city of these dimensions being right here on this earth!

Three
Bodies of Flesh and Bone

I want to present in human language, if possible, some of the beauty, glory, and reality of heaven. Mark it down that heaven is very, very real. This reality is its most wonderful quality. We are going to have real bodies and take up real activities. In fact, in Isaiah 65 we are told that the redeemed will plant vineyards and eat the fruit of them; we are going to build houses, and live in them. "And they shall build houses, and inhabit them; and they shall plant vineyards, and eat the fruit of them. They shall not build, and another inhabit; they shall not plant, and another eat: for as the days of a tree are the days of my people, and mine elect shall long enjoy the work of their hands" (vs. 21, 22).

Now it may surprise you to learn this, but we are going to have bodies of flesh and bone in heaven. That is what the Bible teaches. Two texts will prove this point beyond question. In Philippians 3:21 we read: "Who shall change our vile body, that it may be fashioned like unto his glorious body." How exciting it is to know that our present physical natures will be changed. We will have bodies just like Jesus had after He was resurrected! There is no mystery here because Jesus explained to His disciples all about that body. He said, "Behold my hands and my feet, that it is I myself: handle me, and see; for a spirit hath not flesh and bones, as ye see me have" (Luke 24:39).

First, He appeared to them and said He had flesh and bone. Then He ate with them, and finally, He ascended bodily right out of their midst. This sequence of events in the life of our Lord answers many questions concerning our own nature in the hereafter. We will have a body made like the very same body Jesus possessed after His resurrection.

Four
We Will Know Each Other

This raises another interesting question which has perplexed millions of people: Will we know each other there? Will we be able to recognize one another in the hereafter?

Many people have the misconception that heaven will be very impersonal. The Bible reveals exactly the opposite. Although the former troubles and sorrows will be erased from the mind, we certainly will not forget our friends and family. No one will be known only as an animated number! The truth is that we will know each other better in heaven than we know one another now. Paul wrote, "For now we see through a glass, darkly; but then face to face: now I know in part; but then shall I know even as also I am known" (1 Corinthians 13:12). If I understand the English language at all, this means that we will know one another better when we get up there than we do here. We see things very dimly here, and we misunderstand each other often. This will never happen in the new earth. We will know each other clearly and plainly.

Jesus said that "many shall come from the east and west, and shall sit down with Abraham, and Isaac, and Jacob, in the kingdom of heaven" (Matthew 8:11). Surely this indicates that we will recognize those great stalwarts of the Old Testament. Not only will we be forever united with those we loved on earth, but we can make the acquaintance of those mighty spiritual giants who inspired us from the pages of the Bible.

Most people love reunions and home-comings. What a delight it is to meet old friends after many years and to renew nostalgic ties of the past. Heaven would not be enjoyable if no one recognized anybody else. I have had the joy of leading thousands of people to Christ, and I anticipate meeting them around the throne of God. It is unthinkable that I would never have the assurance that even one of those souls actually held faithful to the end and received the crown of life. We will undoubtedly meet people there who were won to Christ by those we won, and we will be able to see the endless cycle of influence as it vibrated from heart to heart and life to life.

Can't you imagine the thrill of hearing someone say to you in that day, "It was you who influenced me to follow Jesus all the way. Thank you! Oh, thank you for making it possible for me to be here"? Surely that will be a great part of the reward for soul winners.

Paul wrote to the Philippians, "And I entreat thee also, true yokefellow, help those women which labored with me in the gospel, with Clement also, and with other my fellow laborers, whose names are in the book of life" (Philippians 4:3). Here is very interesting evidence that earthly names are recorded in the books of heaven. There is no reason to believe that those faithful workers with Paul received some kind of new, angelic names after they were converted. The very same names were written in the book of life that had been given by their Judean mothers. The same is true today. John, Bob, Tim, Betty, and Dana are faithfully recorded as being worthy of eternal life through faith in Jesus.

We get another insight into this subject in the book of Revelation. In one of his visions, John was shown the glory of the New Jerusalem. It was so dazzling that the prophet was almost overwhelmed by the glory of it. As he drew nearer to the shining walls in his vision, John saw that the foundation of the city was composed of 12 precious stones, all of different colors. Then he saw that a name was inscribed in each of the glittering foundation stones. Imagine his feelings at the moment he recognized his own name on one of those stones! All the apostles will be honored throughout eternity by having their simple Galilean names etched into the massive support stones of the New Jerusalem. What a thrill that must have been for John!

After the New Jerusalem descends to this earth at the end of the thousand years, the earth will be re-created in its original, perfect form. God's dwelling place will be among men, and the saints will dwell in both the city and the new earth. We will have a city home as well as a country estate. The mansion in the New Jerusalem is being prepared right now by Jesus (John 14:1–3). We will build our own house in the country to our own specifications (Isaiah 65:21, 22).

Five
City Mansion and Country Estate

Will we be satisfied with the home Jesus is getting ready for us? He said, "I go to prepare a place for you." I go to prepare a place for whom? For you! You may put your own name in there if you would like, because it is true. He went to get a place ready for you, and your name will be on it. I like that, because the Lord is a builder who knows just exactly what I would like the most.

I believe the Lord will meet each one of us and show us through the Holy City. He will escort us down those golden streets to show us all the different places of interest in the New Jerusalem. We will walk along the river of life, and He will tell us all about the tree of life, which grows over the river and bears a different manner of fruit each month. He will take us down one street after another, and finally, as we move along, we are going to see a certain mansion. As soon as we see it, there will be a responsive chord in our heart and we will think, "My, that's just what I've always wanted. That's the kind of mansion I'd like to have!" And Jesus will interrupt our thoughts and say, "This is yours. I've prepared it exactly as I knew you'd want it. This one is especially for you."

In addition, we will be able to build ourselves a country home. Remember that Isaiah promised we shall build houses and inhabit them? And we can pick our own location. There is the whole beautiful new world before us, and we can find the choicest place that will fit our own personality and put up our house right there. I close my eyes sometimes and try to think of a place that would please me, and I can think of a lot of them that would make me happy. It will be without any spot of sin, for there will be no more curse upon the land. We will never be bothered by thieves or lose the house by fire. I have talked to poor people whose home had burned, destroying their every possession. Others have lost their life's savings to embezzlers and thieves.

Somebody says, "Well, I don't know how to build. I don't think I want to build houses." Listen, don't think it will be the kind of laborious work you see the poor carpenters in this world doing. No, it is not going to be like that at all. As for your knowledge of how to build, don't worry about it for a moment. There will be no limit to what you can learn. You will have a whole eternity before you to learn and understand. If you don't know anything about music, take a music course. Join the heavenly choir. You can go into the bass section one day and learn to sing bass, and then you can go into the tenor section and sing tenor. You can sing all the parts and learn just as much about music as you want to learn.

You can learn architecture. You can learn to build. You can learn about nature. Or maybe you want to study astronomy. Sometimes, when we look up into the heavens and see a little yellow star glimmering in the southwest sky, we say, "My, I wonder what that little star is away up there?" Listen, someday we won't need to wonder; we can just say, "I think I will go and find out." Then we can visit that star. That is what the new earth will be like. We can travel with the speed of light. Angels can do it now. Daniel started praying one day, and before he ended his prayer an angel had come all the way from heaven to his side. The angel said, "Daniel, when you began to pray, God sent me from His throne, and now I'm here in answer to your prayer." We will be able to travel like that. We can go out to visit the great, expansive universe of God and understand things that no human mind has been able to comprehend before.

Oftentimes people ask me if there will be animals in heaven. The Bible has a surprising number of references to this question. Pet lovers will have a field day there! "The wolf also shall dwell with the lamb, and the leopard shall lie down with the kid; and the calf and the young lion and the fatling together; and a little child shall lead them. And the cow and the bear shall feed; their young ones shall lie down together: and the lion shall eat straw like the ox. And the suckling child shall play on the hole of the asp, and the weaned child shall put his hand on the cockatrice den. They shall not hurt nor destroy in all my holy mountain" (Isaiah 11:6–9).

Sometimes we have heard of lions that have been domesticated and will allow children to play on their backs. Too often, though, we have read stories of family pets that suddenly turned upon children, attacking them like wild animals.

The ravages of sin have made animal nature unpredictable at best. But in the restored Eden of God there will be absolutely no danger of violence from lions, leopards, bears, or snakes—much less from the beloved animal pets of earth.

In this world, all of created life has to be on guard against attack at any time. The reign of tooth and claw has created an atmosphere of constant fear in the animal kingdom. Birds seem never relaxed as their heads dart from side-to-side, watching for potential attackers.

Tragically, it is only in that restored paradise that we will be able to relax our own guard against criminal violence from fellow human beings. For the first time since Eden men will be able to trust other men. No one will be there who could inflict harm or unhappiness on any creature.

Six

No Sickness and No Death

Since there will be no sickness, pain, or death, some occupations and professions will be totally out of place. No doctors, nurses, morticians, or insurance agents could find a soul to do business with. Financial problems will be banished forever. The very issues that cause the greatest grief now will not even exist in the minds of the saints. They will forget eternally the troubles of this life.

Won't we grieve for loved ones who are not there? No doubt we will weep when the discovery is made that they are missing, but then God shall wipe all tears from their eyes.

One of the greatest promises in the Bible is found in Revelation 21:3, 4. "And I heard a great voice out of heaven saying, Behold, the tabernacle of God is with men, and he will dwell with them, and they shall be his people, and God himself shall be with them, and be their God. And God shall wipe away all tears from their eyes; and there shall be no more death, neither sorrow, nor crying, neither shall there be any more pain: for the former things are passed away." Isn't that wonderful? I tell you, if heaven were no more than these two verses describe, I'd want to be there! Wouldn't you? No more cause for sorrow—no pain, no death, no separation.

In Isaiah 33:24 we read something else about the people who will live in that new world: "And the inhabitant shall not say, I am sick." Sometimes when I meet people on Sabbath morning I ask, "How are you today?" And every once in a while someone says, "I'm not feeling very well. I probably should have stayed in bed." Well, maybe they should have, but they loved the Lord so much that they wanted to come out to His house of worship. Yes, people here get sick, but in heaven we'll never have to use that expression. It will be done away with altogether. We will never even ask, "How are you this morning?" We will know how they are. They are fine. They are not sick. They feel perfect. The immortal bloom of youth will be upon every face. No one will say, "I am sick." No one will feel the desperation of seeing loved ones suffer and then slip over the brink into death.

Oh, I long for this experience more than for anything else. Children will be safe in this new kingdom God is preparing for us. Let me tell you this, parents, and you may take great comfort from it—your children will never be in danger of getting hit with automobiles. I will never forget the scene in front of the tent in our Louisville crusade. Right in the middle of the street I saw a little girl who had been hit and killed by a car. I have never been able to blot out of my mind the scene of that little girl lying all crumpled up.

The Bible says children will be there, and they are going to play in the streets and never get hurt. "And the streets of the city shall be full of boys and girls playing in the streets thereof" (Zechariah 8:5). Won't that be wonderful? Parents, have you ever heard squealing automobile brakes that made you freeze in your tracks? Then you ran to the window with your heart in your mouth to see whether your child was in the street? You have done that more than once, haven't you? But there will be no fear that your children are not safe in the new earth. And even when they play alongside the river of life, you are not going to be worried about them at all. They will not fall in and drown. "They shall not hurt nor destroy in all my holy mountain, saith the Lord" (Isaiah 65:25).

Children are going to grow up there. The Bible says they will grow up as calves in the stall, and I think we adults are going to grow up, too. We will grow up spiritually and intellectually.

Now I'm going to say something that I can't prove from the Bible. I can't give you a text for this, so you just take it or leave it; but I think we are going to have a little trouble conversing with Adam in the beginning. He was made in the image of God, and our poor minds have become dull by the inherited tendencies and weaknesses of 6,000 years of sin. We will have to develop quite a bit to catch up with Adam, but we will learn quickly.

No doubt we will grow up physically, too. I'm sure Adam was a lot taller and stronger than any man today. The Bible says there were giants in the earth in those days. One man is described in the book of Genesis as being 10 feet tall. I can well believe that Adam and Eve were 12 or 15 feet tall. I believe the entire, final curse of sin will be taken away as we grow up into the image of God, as it was reflected in Adam and Eve. What a transcending thrill it will be to walk up to this great big giant of a man and put out my hand and say, "My name is Crews." Adam will put his hand down and look at me like a child and say, "Well, I'm Adam." I want to get acquainted with Adam.

Writing in the context of the end of all things, Malachi said: "But unto you that fear my name shall the Sun of righteousness arise with healing in his wings; and ye shall go forth, and grow up as calves of the stall" (Malachi 4:2). We often interpret this to mean that parents can watch their children grow into holy adulthood, but could it not also apply to all of us as we grow out of the stunting effects of sin? Although we cannot be dogmatic on this point, it seems likely that this could happen.

All defects will be left behind when we go there. In Isaiah 35:5, 6 we have a beautiful promise: "Then the eyes of the blind shall be opened, and the ears of the deaf shall be unstopped. Then shall the lame man leap as an hart, and the tongue of the dumb sing: for in the wilderness shall waters break out, and streams in the desert." One of the greatest joys will be to hear voices on every side saying, "I can see again!" and "I can hear!" and "I'm strong!" All the infirmities of old age will disappear forever and ever, and we will see only the bloom of eternal youth. Every mind will be keen and alert.

While living in India I often saw heartbreaking scenes of human suffering and human wretchedness. Beggars lined the streets in certain places—crippled, twisted in body and mind, leprous, and blind. Not even a memory or reminder of such an experience will afflict the inhabitants of this glorious earth made new.

The Bible says, "They shall run, and not be weary; and they shall walk, and not faint" (Isaiah 40:31). With bodies that will never tire we may explore the majestic expanse of the City of God. It will take only a tiny fragment of eternity to traverse every street of that New Jerusalem with its 1,500-mile wall of purest jasper. Every square inch of this reconstituted planet will scintillate with the rarest beauty and appeal. Those who love to travel will find heaven a special place. The entire unfallen universe will be open to our study and observation. We will be able to visit the billions of exciting planets, solar systems, and galaxies that were never spoiled by the touch of sin. We may go where we like, stay as long as we please, and return as quick as a flash. Is anything more wonderful to contemplate?

Maybe you are interested in people, as I am. Have you ever thought of the joy of getting acquainted with folk you have read about in the Bible? In my library is a book in which a man tries to explain on a natural basis how Noah got all those animals into that ark. I can't quite understand the man who tries to explain it, but I would like to sit down with Noah and talk to him; wouldn't you? That is what we will do some day. We will be able to ask him about it and find out just how he did get all those animals in, and how they stayed for over a year.

Then, I have thought about Abraham and that terrible day when he took his own son, at God's order, to kill him on top of Mt. Moriah. Oh, what an experience that must have been for Abraham! I have tried to imagine what that father felt as he toiled up the side of the mountain, knowing that with his own hand he had to kill his beloved son. Someday I want to ask Abraham about that awful experience, and he will explain just what it meant when he was about to take his own son's life.

Then, I want to talk to the centurion who stood by and saw Jesus crucified—the one who said, "Truly, this was the Son of God." I'd like to know more of the details of that terrible day, wouldn't you? And, mothers, wouldn't you like to talk to Mary? Thirty years of Jesus' life we know nothing about. Wouldn't you like to ask Mary about Jesus as a child and as a youth?

Even in our wildest imagination we find it difficult to envision those special contacts with Bible characters we have learned to love and respect. Nevertheless, it is thrilling to anticipate how it will be when we actually meet them.

Seven
Unimaginable Beauty and Happiness

In 1 Corinthians 2:9 we are told, "Eye hath not seen, nor ear heard, neither have entered into the heart of man, the things which God hath prepared for them that love him." Now, to me that is a promise without parallel. There is nothing quite like it in all the Bible. When it says that I have never seen anything to compare with heaven, that is great enough, because I have seen some wonderful things in this world.

I have visited many countries and I've seen things I have felt to be absolutely unsurpassed. I saw the beautiful Taj Mahal in India. I have seen the towering mountains of Switzerland and the lovely tulip gardens of Holland, but heaven will be immeasurably more beautiful than any of those sights. Some of my friends went up into the vale of Kashmir, over the great passes of the Himalaya Mountains. They tell me that nothing on earth can compare with those beautiful valleys!

Some friends of mine in Pakistan went out into the Shangri-La country of Hunza, and they told me about the placid lakes and the beautiful mountains. It sounded wonderful; but, listen—the Bible says we have never heard about anything that would give us even the faintest idea of what heaven is really like.

The text goes on to say that we have never even imagined the true beauty of it. It has not entered into the heart of man. I have a fertile imagination and I can imagine things that are just out of this world; but still the Bible says it won't even begin to approach the beauty and glory of heaven.

One of the most pleasing aspects of that holy habitation is that it will be a clean city and a clean country. "And there shall in no wise enter into it any thing that defileth, neither whatsoever worketh abomination, or maketh a lie: but they which are written in the Lamb's book of life" (Revelation 21:27). Can you picture an entire city, much less a planet, in which no foul smell of stale cigarette smoke will ever be known? In that day God will have a limitless universe where no chemical poison can exist. The golden streets will never know the litter of beer cans and tobacco butts. Defiling the body, defiling the air, and defiling the street will be unknown in God's royal capital city.

I grew up near Winston-Salem, North Carolina, and the noisome smell of tobacco hung in the air of those city streets. As one of the world's largest markets for the filthy weed, it exuded the familiar, permeating odor of aging tobacco. What a joy it was to get away from the area where so much natural beauty was negated by the miasma of nicotine pollution.

Later I responded to a mission call to India, and our family located in the beautiful city of Bangalore. After settling into our cozy rented bungalow, an east wind sprang up and we found out what lay on the other side of the red wall across the street. A tobacco factory!

For a few more years we had to endure the unpleasant odor of the processed poison.

After returning to the United States I responded to an invitation to pastor a church in Louisville, Kentucky. Just as we crossed over the city line our nostrils were assailed by a very familiar smell. Tobacco again! But this time it was combined with the stench of fermented alcohol. Louisville, we discovered, was famous for its tobacco and distilleries. I am now convinced that there can be no real relief from these corrupting influences until I take up residence in that clean city of New Jerusalem.

We have alluded to many of the dramatic changes in lifestyle that will mark those who inherit the new earth. We have tried to portray in human language the joy and delight of dwelling in a perfect environment, free from all sin and its despoiling influence. Each circumstance has been challenging and exciting. It makes us eager to leave this vale of tears as soon as possible.

Our senses are stirred by the prospect of such physical benefits as no sickness, no pain, and no death. Yet the very highest pleasure reserved for the redeemed will have nothing to do with their life style, their food, or their immortal nature. The sweetest delight of heaven will be to see Jesus face-to-face and to live with Him throughout eternity. What a prospect! To see the nail prints in His hands, and to open our minds to His own divine instruction in the science of salvation.

Now the question I want to leave with you is this: When that day dawns and the saints of God march into that city, will you be among them? Abraham will be there; Isaac, Jacob, Joseph, Peter, and Paul will march inside the gates. When they are inside, will you be inside, too? We can make a reservation now if we so desire.

During World War II many Americans were caught in Singapore, and even though the American government provided a means of helping them, they had difficulty getting out because of the vicissitudes of war. One day a very fine, well-dressed man walked into the American Embassy and said, "Book me out of here; I want to get out as quickly as possible." The ambassador said, "All right, where is your passport?" The man said "I don't have a passport." The ambassador asked, "Aren't you a citizen?" He said, "Well, no, I really never did take out any papers, but I've lived there all my life. I have a business over there, and my bank account is there, and I love America. I'm an American." The ambassador said, "I'm sorry, but I can't do a thing for you. If you are not a citizen, I can't help you." The man went away sick with disappointment.

A little while later another man came walking in, dressed in old, shabby clothes. He spoke with a heavy accent as he asked to be booked up to leave on the next plane. The ambassador asked, "Where are your papers?" The man replied, "Here they are. I had them taken out just before I left America." And the ambassador put out his hand and said, "All the power of the United States government will stand behind you in getting out to safety."

Both of those men loved America very much. Both of them claimed to be Americans, but only one of them had his papers; only one had his passport. Only one of them could make a reservation. And you can make reservations if you want to, but you must be a citizen of that heavenly kingdom before you can do it. If you want to do it, you can make your reservation right now. When that day comes, you can join with God's people of all the ages and dwell in this beautiful city under the ideal conditions that we have described. You must not miss it.